Bitchen'
IN THE
Kitchen
JANINE DETORE

From My Big Family To Your Table

COPYRIGHT

Wahida Clark Presents Innovative Publishing
60 Evergreen Place Suite 904
East Orange, NJ 07018
1-866-910-6920
wclarkpublishing.com

www.janinedetore.com

Copyright 2021 © by Janine Detore

Bitchen' in The Kitchen: From my BIG Family to Your Table

Library of Congress Control Number: 2021913397

ISBN 13-digit 978-1-954161-36-8 (Paperback)
ISBN 13-digit 978-1-954161-37-5 (E-book)
ISBN 13 digit 978-1-954161-38-2 (Audiobook)
ISBN 13 digit 978-1-954161-32-0 (Hardback)

Library of Congress Catalog Number: 2021904281

1. Italian Cooking
2. Family Friendly
3. Gourmet Cooking (Books)
4. Cooking Encyclopedias
5. Entertaining & Holiday Cooking

Art Direction by Nuance Art LLC
Book Layout & Design by Destiny Augustine
wahida@visualsweetness.com

Printed in United States

DEDICATIONS

To my seven beautiful children: Louis, John, Allie, Baby Dom, Jeannie, Sonnie, and baby Ronnie; never forget the love I have for all of you. You have all taught me something special and for that, thank you. No one else will ever know the strength of my love for you all. After all, you're the only seven who know what my heart sounds like from the inside!

To my three beautiful granddaughters Savannah, Audrianna AKA "Cheffy", and Joelle; you girls taught me how to smile again. I love you all with every fiber of my being.

To my kids' significant others: thank you for loving my children as much as I do... (well, maybe a little less). I love sharing them with you.

To my sisters, brothers, nieces, nephews, in-laws, cousins, and my very best friends. Thank you for always being there; especially my sister Donna, who helps me when she can. Even though I yell and scream at you, I'm always grateful for all your help.

To my sister Angela, thank you for taking me on your journey. I love being your sister and best friend. You made it, Angela, and it was big. Please watch over us. I miss you so very much.

Last, but never least...my partner in crime, the man who has to shake my pans, or he's not happy. Thank you for giving me this life. The life I always dreamt of...YOU ARE MY BIGGEST FAN AND BIGGEST SUPPORTER, MY HEART. What would I do without you? I hope I never have to find out. I love you tremendously. This ride is always fun with you; thank you for loving me so much, even when I didn't love myself.

I love your crazy ideas, Ralph. If you watched the Honeymooners, you'd get this, and this book is about us! What we have created together. The most wonderful children. Thank you for loving them like you do. I couldn't have picked a better father than you!

I LOVE YOU, DOM .... THE LOVE OF YOUR LIFE!
YOUR WIFE

And a special thanks to Deana. Thank you for all the support through the years and for helping me organize all these recipes. I couldn't have done it without you!

A personal thank you to Jesse at Syndicate Productions, who helped bring my recipes alive.

And a special thank you to Mike Joseph MNJ Images on Staten Island for all your hard work and fantastic pictures!

Thank you Mike Sword for being there through everything!

And a special thank you to my publisher, Wahida Clark Publishing, owned by Wahida Clark. Thank you Wahida, Nuance, Tashiyanna, Caroline, and Chris.

TABLE OF CONTENT

A NOTE FROM ME TO YOU

These recipes mean a lot to me because it brings me back to my childhood. A time when my family would get together every night and enjoy my mom's homemade meals! Family time is becoming a thing of the past, and that makes me very sad. When my mom cooked... you were at the table... that's it! There was no discussion or excuses... YOU WERE THERE!

We, as a country, are losing this wonderful family time. I need to bring you back to the table with your husbands, wives, partners, children, and in-laws. You need to see how their day was and talk about yours!

I truly believe we can all sit as a family and discuss things like our jobs... our everyday lives, and school friends. If something is bothering us, or someone is bullying us... we can save ourselves a lot of heartache!

We must try to get our families and friends back to the old-fashioned times.... the "old school way" is the only way! We are so involved in our cell phones, video games, and texting that we are losing sight of what's really important and that's right in front of us!

I think if I can be (clears throat) 55 years old, run a business, take care of ten plus people daily, cook, do the laundry, clean, shop, design rhinestones... and be Dominick's wife/girlfriend... I've done MY job.

Let me teach you how to get back to these wonderful family traditions. It makes memories, and let's face it... we aren't going to be around forever. So, I want to leave my memory to my kids, grandkids, and in-laws, among others.

That way, when they see a certain thing or smell a certain meal... they'll say... "ohhhh, remember that day Mom made us this?"

"Wow, I miss her so much!"
Because I know I'll sure miss them. I love you all.

Always remember that I made these recipes and these traditions for you to carry on when I'm not here.

PREFACE

This is Bitchen' in the Kitchen with your favorite cook... me!

My family is the most important thing to me, and through the years, because of technology and less family time, I must admit it breaks my heart. My cookbook is meant to fix that problem that we find ourselves in every night. We're going to bring our families back together like it was when we were growing up.

Everyone is always busy, but if you make the food before you go to work, this will bring them back to the table without all the other distractions. No phones, no rush, just one hour over a great meal to talk about your day.

Family has taken a back seat to technology, television, and the everyday hustle we all go through.

And you know what? At the end of the day, all we got is family.

In my house, we want to make memories with our children. We want our children to remember Dom and me. When they walk past a pot roast or a meatball, all the ingredients that are in here they'll say, "Man, I wish I could taste that dish one more time."

Everything we do, we do for them.

Janine Detore

Aunt Marie's Sweet & Sour Pork Chops

This recipe was created by my sister-in-law Marie (My brother Stephen's wife). She goes by the IG handle... Eggplant Mama. She walked me through the recipe. It's quick and easy and just goes in the oven. I promise it won't come out like an old leather shoe. Marie and I like to call it Asian/Italian Fusion. Enjoy!

Serves 8

Prep Time: 25mins
Cook Time: 4-5hrs

1 cup of oil for frying
8 bone-in pork chops
6 eggs (or egg beaters- my preference)
2 cups of breadcrumbs
8 red, orange, or yellow peppers
1 Jalapeno pepper (if you want a little spicy-you only need about four small slices)
3 large yellow onions
1 ½ cups of grated Pecorino/Romano cheese blend (I like Locatelli)
1 cup of soy sauce
1 jar of duck sauce
Salt and pepper to taste

Instructions

1. Preheat oven to 250 degrees.
2. Slice all the peppers and remove the seeds. Then cut the long way down to make strips.
3. Cut onions up into strips or thin slices. Place aside.
4. Put eggs or egg beaters in a bowl. Add salt, pepper, and cheese blend.
5. Put breadcrumbs on a large plate or pan.
6. Take each pork chop and dip in egg mixture and then the breadcrumbs. Coat evenly.
7. Heat oil until it's hot. Use about 1 to 1 ½ inches of oil. The chops will not fry up well if you put them in cold oil to start.
8. Take another pan and add a little bit of oil about ½ inch for the peppers and onions.
9. When the oil is warm for the peppers and onions, mix them together and pile them into the pan. Cook until soft.
10. Place & fry chops in hot oil for few minutes, then turn them. You want both sides golden brown.
11. When chops are golden, put them in a large baking pan.
12. Shortly before the peppers and onions are done, pour soy sauce & duck sauce in the pan over them.
13. Use a medium to large jar of duck sauce (again, this all depends on how many chops you are making. For 8 chops, I use a 40 oz jar of Dai Day duck sauce).
14. Cook a little longer. When onions and peppers are soft, remove from heat. Give it a taste to make sure it's to your liking.
15. Pour onions, peppers, soy sauce, and duck sauce mixture all over the chops that are in the baking pan. Spread evenly.
16. Take aluminum foil and seal baking pan. Make sure you use about two to three layers to make a tight seal.
17. Place in oven and cook several hours (4-5). I know you won't believe it, but they will be falling apart. The juice from the pork chops over the Rice Pilaf "Detore Style" is the best thing you've ever had. Enjoy!

Grandma Jean's Pork Chops with Vinegar Peppers

My mother taught this recipe to me in 1978. I was twelve years old. I guarantee you will need a few loaves of Italian bread for everyone at the table. Follow the recipe exactly, or you'll get a chop that is as tough as Rocky Balboa!

And just so you know, it's a myth that you can't leave a pork a little pink... NOT TRUE. Pan sear each side for a minute, finish in a pan with juice. No more than 5-7 minutes to make it perfect.

Prep Time: 15mins
Cook Time: 20mins

8 bone in pork chops
5 fresh garlic cloves, chopped
Salt and pepper
1-2 cans of College Inn chicken broth
1 jar of sweet peppers in vinegar (you can also use hot if that's what you like,
or you can mix both. I use B & G brand peppers)
½ cup Olive oil

Instructions

1. Pour peppers in a bowl. Take the peppers and pull apart, removing the seeds. Then rip any big pepper pieces into smaller pieces. Save the juice!
2. Chop up a good amount of garlic.
3. Place a little bit of olive oil in a pan.
4. Heat oil and add garlic.
5. Sauté the garlic until it starts turning golden brown.
6. Pour the peppers into the pan over the garlic and mix well. Add salt and pepper to taste.
7. Let cook for 5 to 7 minutes.
8. Use 1 can of College Inn chicken broth. Shake can well and add 1 can of the College Inn chicken broth and the juice from the peppers. The broth "cuts" the vinegar flavor so it's not so strong. If you need more, add it.
9. Mix again and keep on the heat.
10. Take the pork chops and sprinkle salt and pepper on them. Pan sear them very quickly on both sides. Don't overcook it. It is okay to have a LITTLE pink inside.
11. Take the pan-seared pork chops and place in the pan with pepper/chicken broth/pepper juice mix that's still cooking. Let it absorb for about 15 minutes or so.
12. Serve immediately with your favorite side. You definitely want to serve this with hot Italian bread to dip in the juice. Delish!

Sister Donna's Cauliflower Au Gratin

My sister Donna absolutely loves this side dish... it just hits the spot between meals, or you can serve it at dinner. It's quick and easy to make fresh as soon as you get home from work, so it's hot and fresh for your kids.

2 heads of cauliflower trimmed and cut to small florets, or you can use two bags of frozen cauliflower.

Prep Time: 35mins
Cook Time: 45mins OR until Golden Brown

Sauce:
½ stick of sweet butter
1 tbsp garlic, minced
3 tbsp flour
2 cups milk
½ cup heavy cream
Salt, pepper and nutmeg to taste
1-2 tbsp white Truffle oil
8 oz. shredded gruyere cheese

Topping:
1 cup Panko breadcrumbs
2 tbsp melted butter
Paprika to taste

Instructions

1. Sauté the garlic for one minute and add the flour. Cook for 2 more minutes. Whisk in milk, cook an additional 5 minutes. Add heavy cream, seasonings and truffle oil.
2. Cook cauliflower until tender in water, then drain (or follow package directions if using frozen).
3. Mix the cauliflower into the sauce and put in the cooking pan. Top with the cheese.
4. Mix Panko with butter and paprika and sprinkle over cheese and cauliflower.
5. Bake at 400 degrees until golden brown.

Rice Pilaf "Detore Style"

This is another great side dish of mine. We ate a lot of Rice-A-Roni as kids. We loved it, but we wanted to make it "Detore" style in my kitchen, and it is Bitchen'!

Serves 8-10   **Prep Time: 5-10mins**
Cook Time: 40mins

3 tbsp olive oil
3 tbsp butter
1 large shallot, finely chopped
1 clove garlic
½ cup orzo macaroni
2 cups jasmine rice
4 cups College Inn chicken broth
sautéed mushrooms (optional)

Instructions
1. Heat oil and butter in saucepan.
2. Add shallots and cook for 5 minutes.
3. Add garlic and orzo macaroni and cook until the macaroni is golden brown.
4. Add rice and sauté for 5 minutes.
5. Add College Inn chicken broth and bring to a boil, cover until macaroni & rice are fluffy.
6. Reduce heat to a simmer and cook for 20 minutes.
7. Add mushrooms if using them and fluff rice with fork.

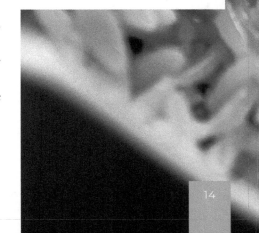

Johnny Boy's
Chicken Francese

When I was in my twenties, I started paying closer attention to what my mother was doing in the kitchen. I mean, I had always been there, but some recipes are easier than others. In fact, one holiday dinner, me, Angela, and my daughter Jeannie went to my brother Louis' house. Louis made Brains Francese. My sister Angela downed it in one sitting, and Jeannie even tasted it. I sure as Hell wasn't going to eat it... ugh...

Serves 8-10

Prep Time: 40mins
Cook Time: 20mins

2 lbs. chicken cutlets, pounded
2 ½ cups of flour
6 eggs
½ cup of milk
1 cup of Pecorino Romano cheese
¼ to ½ tbsp of parsley
2 cloves of garlic, finely minced
Salt and pepper to taste
¼ cup of olive oil

Sauce:
1 stick of butter
3 cloves minced garlic
½ cup flour
2 cups chicken broth
1 cup freshly squeezed lemon juice
¼ cup finely chopped parsley
1 lb. sautéed mushrooms

Instructions

1. Start heating oil in pan.
2. Mix milk and eggs, cheese, parsley, salt and pepper and garlic together in a shallow bowl.
3. Coat the chicken with the flour, then dip into the egg mixture.
4. Immediately sauté in a pan with oil over medium heat.
5. Drain on rack.
6. Remove oil from pan and add butter and garlic.
7. Sauté garlic and mushrooms for about 3 minutes until slightly brown.
8. Add chicken broth and lemon juice and simmer for about 7 minutes on low heat.
9. Add flour & water to thicken the sauce and cook for 5 minutes.
10. Add salt and pepper to taste.
11. Then add chicken and let simmer for 5 more minutes until done.

Tastes best with my Rice Pilaf "Detore Style"

AJ's Favorite Pot Roast

I started to make this dish when I worked at a PS 45 (Public School) where I was a school aide in 2005. It was difficult to be a mom and a full-time worker, so I used to put it in the crock pot, go to work, come home and serve it.

Serves 8-10

Prep Time: 20mins
Cook Time: 4hrs

Use one 4-5 lb. roast (preferably chuck)
2 tsp of salt
1 tsp pepper
1 tsp garlic powder
1 tsp onion powder
½ tsp of celery seed
2 carrots
2 stalks of celery, chopped
1 medium onion, chopped
2 tbsp tomato paste
1 package of dry onion soup mix
4 cups of strong beef stock
2 bay leaves
2 tbsp oil

Instructions

1.   Rub spice blend on all sides of roast and then brown in Dutch oven in oil.
2.   Remove browned roast from pot and add carrots, celery, and onion to pot and brown for 5 minutes.
3.   Return roast to pot. Add tomato paste and cook another 5 minutes.
4.   Add bay leaves and simmer on low for four hours, turning roast once after 2 hours.
5.   Remove roast and bay leaves from pot and blend the leftover liquid with the vegetables until smooth.
       Thicken with a flour and water slurry if needed to reach desired consistency of gravy.

Lucky #7 Ronnie's Chili

This is the dish we make for Super Bowl Sunday and a lot during the winter. It's quick and filling. Why not, right? Our favorite football team is the San Francisco 49ers because me and Dom have some friends who we bet with one night. When we won, we all started singing, "We going Sizzlers, we going Sizzlers!"

This wasn't when we were young, either. I had 5 kids then, too. This is not only good plain, it's good on hot dogs.

2 lbs. ground beef
1 large chopped onion
2 cloves garlic, minced
1-2 Jalapeno peppers, finely diced
3 tbsp chili powder
1 tbsp cumin
1 can of stewed tomatoes
1 can of tomato sauce
2 cups of water with 2 beef bouillon cubes
3 cans of mixed beans drained and rinsed (I use pinto, red kidney and black beans)
2 bay leaves
Shredded cheddar cheese
Sour cream (if desired)
Add some crushed up Fritos on top, too

Instructions

1. Brown and crumble beef.
2. Drain but reserve 2 tbsp of the fat.
3. Brown onion, garlic and peppers with the spices.
4. Add browned beef.
5. Add remaining ingredients with 2 bay leaves.
6. Add salt and pepper to taste.
7. Simmer on low heat for at least 2 hours.
8. Adjust seasoning and liquid ingredients to liking.

I top with diced onion, shredded cheese, diced jalapeño and sour cream. I also serve it with white rice.

Allie's Delicious Butternut Squash Soup

I can eat soup 365 days a year. It doesn't matter if it's 100 degrees outside. It is mine and Angela's favorite food. Any soup... anywhere... anytime. Just like in Seinfeld. "No soup for you!"

Prep Time: 30mins
Cook Time: 1hr-30mins

3 tbsp butter
3 chopped carrots
3 stalks of chopped celery
1 chopped parsnip
2 cloves of minced garlic
2 lbs. of cubed butternut squash
2 quarts chicken or vegetable stock
2 cups of water
2 bay leaves
¼ cup of flour
2 cups of heavy cream

Instructions
1. Sauté carrots, celery, parsnips, and garlic in butter for 10 minutes.
2. Add stock and water and bring to a simmer. Simmer for 15 minutes.
3. Add squash and bay leaves. Simmer until vegetables are tender, about 30 minutes.
4. Puree vegetables and broth in blender until very smooth. Remove bay leaves.
5. Return soup to pot.
6. Mix flour into a cup of water (make sure there are no lumps).
7. Add flour and water mix to pot and simmer for 15 minutes until thickened.
8. Remove from heat.
9. Add cream and salt and pepper to taste.

Lombardi's
Sausage Stuffing

I refuse to stuff the chicken/turkey cavity because the blood drips on it. Yuck... at my house, we bake our stuffing in a pan. My mother and father used to stuff the cavity. But that ain't me, NO WAY!

Serves 14-20

Prep Time: 50mins (including 30mins to soak the bread)
Cook Time: 50mins - 1hr (plus 15mins to set before serving)

1 loaf of stale Italian bread, cubed
3 cups of chicken broth
1 ½ lbs. of sweet Italian sausage, removed from casings
1 medium onion, chopped
3 stalks of celery, chopped
2 garlic cloves, finely minced
½ lb. of grated mozzarella
1 cup of grated Pecorino Romano cheese
1 tsp of dried thyme leaves
2 beaten eggs

Instructions

1. Preheat oven to 350 degrees.
2. Soak bread in chicken stock for about half an hour.
3. Put in strainer and squeeze out excess moisture.
4. Crumble sausage and brown with garlic.
5. Add onion and celery and cook until slightly soft. Do not overcook onion and celery.
6. Mix thoroughly and taste for seasoning.
7. Add salt and pepper as necessary.
8. Take it off stove. Add mozzarella, grated cheese, thyme, and bread.
9. Mix it all together. Taste before you put the eggs in. If needed, add cheeses or spices to your liking.
10. Take the two beaten eggs and mix in.
11. Pour mixture into a 9 x 13 pan and bake for 50-60 minutes or until brown. It shouldn't be served until the stuffing is settled. Let set for about 15-20 minutes.

Grandma Connie's Quiche

Serves 14-20

Prep Time: 30mins
Cook Time: 45-55mins

½ pound of diced bacon
¼ pound of cubed ham
1 large onion, chopped
8 oz. Jarlsberg cheese
2 tbsp of flour
¼ tsp of nutmeg (optional)
1 cup of heavy cream
4 eggs well beaten
1 Pillsbury Pie crust in 9- inch pie pan with flute edge

Instructions

1. Preheat oven to 350 degrees.
2. Brown bacon until crisp.
3. Remove from pan with slotted spoon and drain on paper towel.
4. Sauté onion in bacon fat until brown and add to bowl with bacon.
5. Sauté ham in remaining bacon fat and add to bowl with bacon.
6. In another bowl, toss cheese with flour.
7. Add bacon, onion, eggs and cream to bowl with cheese.
8. Salt and pepper to taste.
9. Add nutmeg if you were using it.
10. Add all the mixture to piecrust and bake until set, approximately 45 to 55 minutes.

Note: You may substitute any other vegetables, meat, or cheese to your taste.

Skinny Lou's Chicken Sausage & Peppers

I use chicken sausage from Premio or Natures Organic chicken sausage. You can use any kind you like. There are so many to choose from. My first born, Louis, can eat like twelve links himself. My son loves to tell me, "No pork on my fork!" I'm Italian, so I love pork sausage. But he's my kid, so chicken it is!

Serves 8-10

Prep Time: 15mins
Cook Time: 45mins

14 sausages of your choice
3 huge onions
3 red bell peppers
3 yellow bell peppers
4 orange bell peppers
You can also use green peppers
Salt & pepper

Instructions

1. Place your sausage on a cookie sheet and put in the oven on roast at 400 degrees.
2. Slice your peppers and onions, take out all the pepper seeds. In a pan on top of the stove, put olive oil in and wait until hot.
3. Put in peppers. Wait until peppers are a bit soft. Add onions, salt pepper and stir till onions are soft.
4. Cover for about 5-10 minutes.
5. Take off cover and stir fry until brown. Place peppers and onions in the center of a platter and surround with your sausage.

Gramma Mary's Cucuzza & Tomatoes (Side Dish)

Serves 8-10

Prep Time: 15mins
Cook Time: 20mins

One or two large cucuzza's (depending on how much you want to make)
1 large onion, diced
2 cloves of garlic
6 fresh plum tomatoes
Salt and pepper to taste
Olive oil to coat pan approximately ¼ inch or so

Instructions

1. Heat oil until hot.
2. Sauté onion until golden brown, but don't burn.
3. Press garlic through garlic press and add to onion.
4. Cut cucuzza and tomato into small pieces.
5. Add cucuzza and tomato to the onion and garlic and cook until soft.
6. Salt and pepper to taste.
7. Serve hot or warm as a side.

This was taught to me by Gramma Mary. Gramma Mary was my good friend Christina's mother, who has now passed. Gramma Mary was a character, and you wouldn't mess with her. Had she been a guy, she would have been a made man and bodies would've been dropping. She was crazy when it came to food. She had rules in her kitchen! I'm just like her, right?

Sonny Sport's Italian (Mascarpone) Cheesecake

Serves 8-10

Prep Time: 1hr
Cook Time: 1hr

1 tsp of softened butter
½ cup of finely crushed Amaretto or vanilla cookies
2 lbs. of ricotta cheese
1 lb. of mascarpone cheese
1 ½ cups of sugar
6 large eggs
2 egg yolks
2 tbsp of fresh orange zest
¼ cup of heavy cream
2 tsp of vanilla
1 tbsp of orange flower water
Powdered sugar for dusting

Instructions

1. Drain the ricotta cheese in a colander lined with cheesecloth for 30 minutes to one hour.
2. Preheat oven to 350 degrees.
3. Butter a 9-inch spring pan.
4. Coat the pan with the crushed cookies, swirling the pan for a good coat. Dump excess crumbs.
5. Using an electric mixer on medium to low, beat the ricotta, mascarpone and sugar together until smooth.
6. Add eggs, orange zest, cream, vanilla and orange flower water.
7. Mix all until well-blended.
8. Place baking pan on a baking sheet.
9. Pour mixture into pan.
10. Bake for approximately 1 and 1/2 hours.
11. Turn off oven and let cake rest for about 30 minutes.
12. Remove cake from oven and let cool to room temperature on wire rack.
13. Run knife around edge to loosen cake and flip on to a serving plate or container.
14. Chill for several hours and serve with a dusting of the powdered sugar.

My father made this recipe. He was a serious cook in the kitchen. Even if we had cell phones, he would have thrown them through the wall... just to prove a point of family first. Let's take our homes back from all technological advancements.

Meatloaf ala Joelle

Serves 12-16

Prep Time: 20mins
Cook Time: 1hr

2 lbs. of chopped beef
3 lbs. of chopped pork
6 cans of tomato sauce
4 cloves of garlic, peeled and put through the garlic press
One whole onion, grated
3 different grated cheeses (your choice)
Breadcrumbs
Egg beaters (you can use eggs, I prefer egg beaters)
Salt and pepper to taste

Instructions

1. Mix all ingredients in a large bowl.
2. Mix with your hands! Don't be afraid to get dirty!
3. The mixture has to be smooth and moist.
4. If it isn't, start adding more tomato sauce or more egg beaters.
5. Shape into a loaf and bake in oven at 350 degrees for about two hours.

This usually makes 2 meatloaves. I usually do one plain and then the other I jazz up. One way I do it is to take bacon and weave it on top of one meatloaf like a basket shape. Another way I do one is to "frost" one with mashed potatoes. I've also been known to hide a boiled egg in one.

Have fun with it! In my opinion, this meatloaf recipe is the best I've ever had. My mom could make great meatloaf... but sorry, Mom!
Mine is the best!

Aunt Ang & Sonnie "Bunnies" Special Pesto

In July of 2013 I got sick and not one doctor knew what I had! I woke up one morning and had lumps on my both knees that were so hot and I couldn't walk. Angela was filming Miami Monkey in Florida at the time.

Dom and the kids had created a vegetable garden on the property next door. They grew tomatoes, zucchini, basil, etc....I called Angela and said I don't think I'm gonna make the night...I felt like death. But the very next day I woke up to Angela sitting at the end of the couch.

I couldn't get upstairs to my bed...so I slept on the living room couch. But there she was, as always...and I always knew I could depend on her. AND THERE SHE WAS ALL THE WAY FROM FLORIDA!

So, after we talked, she and Sonnie went next door to the garden to pick vegetables like you see in this picture.

Angela is allergic to mosquitos...and she came back with over fifteen bites. The welts were everywhere, but that didn't stop her. She taught Sonnie (then age 13) many things that day and one was their special pesto...so enjoy making their recipe.

Everyone should have a person like my sister. The one that whenever or wherever she is, she will come for you.

1 box of farfalle macaroni (depending on the size of your family)
2 cups of fresh basil leaves, packed (you can substitute half the basil leaves with baby spinach)
½ cup of freshly grated Romano or Parmesan cheese (about 2 ounces)
½ cup of extra virgin olive oil
1/3 cup of pine nuts (you can substitute chopped walnuts)
3 cloves of garlic, minced (about 1 tablespoon)
¼ tsp of salt, or more to taste
1/8 tsp of freshly ground black pepper, or more to taste

Instructions

1. Drain the cook farfalle.
2. Place the basil leaves and pine nuts into the bowl of a food processor and pulse several times.
3. Add the garlic and cheese.
4. Slowly pour the olive oil in.
5. Season the pesto sauce by adding salt and freshly ground black pepper.
6. Toss with the drained pasta.

Suggestion: You can do a ton of things and serve it weekly at the table to liven it up and the kids will still get the veggies. So, you can pour the sauce over baked potatoes, or spread it on some crackers during football season...or toasted slices of Italian bread.

Big Ang's Puttanesca
Done My Way

We are good friends with Daymond John from Shark Tank and his wife, Heather. They were having their annual Christmas party, and I was planning on making fish. Dominick told me that our friend, Kiki, who would be at the party, doesn't eat fried fish. So, I got to thinking, what can I do with this fish?

Kiki LOVED it. Everyone did. There were dishes of all kinds of things out for the party and that fish didn't last long at all. People kept asking me how I did it.

Well, this is how. I hope you like it just as much!

Take any fish you like. I use cod, but you could use halibut, swordfish, lemon sole, monkfish or maybe even tuna. I wouldn't use red snapper or salmon.

Prep Time: 30mins
Cook Time: 20-25mins

Make the sauce with:

1 large sliced red onion
4 cloves of chopped garlic
12 Caper Berries
Olive oil
4 oz. of red cherry tomatoes chopped in half
½ cup of cured olives
Drained Kalamata olives
½ cup of Drained green olives...no pimentos
1 stick of butter
Red pepper flakes
Salt and pepper to taste
1 can of College Inn chicken broth
½ cup of white wine (optional)
3 bouillon chicken cubes

Instructions

1.   In a skillet, sauté your sliced red onion & your chopped garlic until soft, don't burn.
2.   Put in cherry tomato halves and sauté until they're a little soft.
3.   Add all 3 olives, salt, pepper, red pepper flakes, stick of butter, & capers. Make sure you strain olives and capers. Stir for 5 minutes.
4.   Add white wine & chicken broth & chicken cubes, continue to stir.
5.   Add fish of your choice. Cover till fish is white.

Suggestion: You can put this over macaroni or you can grill chicken and pour this over it. This recipe can be used for so many other things... it's light and delish! GIVE IT A TRY!

P.S. I taught Madonna (my daughter-in-law) how to make this and she honestly does a good job.

The Raiolas' Fusilli with Genovese Sauce

Serves 8-10

Prep Time: 40mins
Cook Time: 6-7hrs

2 lbs. of long Fusilli macaroni (telephone wire long)
Olive oil
10 to 20 lbs. of onions (yes, you read that correctly)
12 Beef bouillon cubes
Dry basil
3 lbs. of beef
3 lbs. of veal
3 lbs. of pork or 12 sausage links
Horseradish
Red pepper
Salt and pepper to taste

Instructions

1. Cut up onions into strips.
    ONION CUTTING TIP: Put a small piece of white bread in the roof of your mouth and the onions won't make you cry.
2. Get a large pot and add some olive oil to it. Heat the oil and start sautéing all the meat until brown.
3. Add onions. They will start to become translucent and make a lot of water.
4. When onions are see-through, put in beef bouillon cubes.
5. Add red pepper, and salt and pepper to taste.
6. Add basil.
7. Add water until meat is covered, then simmer for 6 to 7 hours.
8. Cook fusilli according to package directions prior to taking meat out.
9. Serve with the cooked macaroni.
10. Serve the meat with horseradish if you choose to. Delish!

My father, Sonny, cooked this. Now I'm the only one that cooks it in the entire family. I always need to give it to my family when I cook it. I should start charging... They take my Tupperware and don't even bring it back... Bastards. Can you believe that? My father taught it to me in my twenties and it's one of my favorite memories.

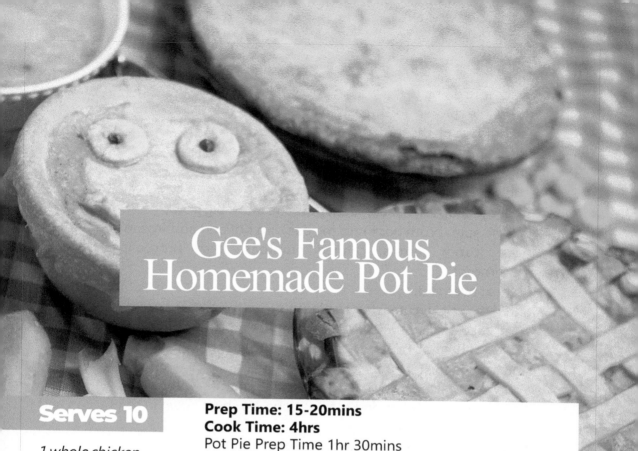

Gee's Famous Homemade Pot Pie

Serves 10

Prep Time: 15-20mins
Cook Time: 4hrs
Pot Pie Prep Time 1hr 30mins
Pot Pie Cook Time 25mins OR Until Golden Brown

1 whole chicken
2-3 chicken breasts
8 fresh Carrots
8 celery stalks
2 large white onions
12 chicken bouillon cubes
8 oz. bag of corn (frozen)
8 oz. bag of peas (frozen)
3 cans of sliced potatoes OR 4 potatoes
8 oz. bag of carrots (frozen)
2 medium cartons of fresh mushrooms
2 heads of fresh broccoli
Actually, you can use whatever vegetables you like
Salt and pepper to taste
Wondra flour
3 Pillsbury pie crusts
Cooking spray, like Pam
3 9-inch cake pans

Instructions

1. First, we're going to make a big pot of chicken soup.
2. Put whole chicken and breasts in pot.
3. Peel and cut up the fresh carrots.
4. Put in onion and celery but leave whole.
5. Put in bouillon cubes and let cook for 4 hours.
6. Add salt and pepper.
7. After the soup is finished, strain the soup into a big bowl.
8. Put the soup broth back into the cooking pot and add frozen corn, frozen peas, frozen carrots, canned potatoes, fresh broccoli, and fresh mushrooms.
9. Preheat oven to 350.
10. Shred the chicken breasts into pieces.
11. Next, take a glass with cold water and start adding Wondra flour to it, mixing until smooth. This is going to thicken up the soup mixture.
12. Add to soup mixture until it's to your liking.
13. Spray your baking pan with cooking spray and coat with flour.
14. Cool the soup mixture and then put one pie sheet down in baking pan and add chicken, soup and veggie mix.
15. Add your other pie crust sheet over top and cut slits in it.
16. Put pies on a baking sheet to help with overflow while cooking.
17. Cook till golden brown.
18. Take out of oven and cool for a few minutes before serving.

I always make chicken soup. I was thinking of what I could do with the leftovers, and so Pot Pie was born. Angela loved my soups.

Uncle Dom's Fried Pizza

This is Dominick's specialty around the house! When Dominick was eighteen, he owned a pizzeria on New Utrecht Avenue and 79th Street in Brooklyn called D & D Pizza. This is how Dominick tells it:

"I was in the pizzeria and just finished making pizza dough. I had a very small piece left over and flattened it. I turned and went to my deep fryer and started making a calzone. When my father walked in and asked how things were going, I told him the dough was done and that I had to wash my hands.

I asked him to watch the calzone that was frying. When I came back from the bathroom, the small piece of extra dough was in the deep fryer. I told my father that it looked like a mini pizza. We took it out and added sauce and mozzarella. My father and I ate it, and to our surprise, it was great!!! Every Friday after that, we made it for our lunch. One of my favorite memories with Dad."

So, in the words of Tony D from Staten Island Hustle... Abbondanza!!!!!

Prep Time: 20-25mins
Cook Time: 3mins (1.5mins on each side)

4 pizza doughs (bought or made)
2 cans of marinara sauce
1 cup of grated cheese (your choice)
Pepperoni
1 lb. of Soppressata (salami like meat)
1 lb. of crumbled sausage
It's really whatever meat or toppings you like on pizza
Oil, either canola or vegetable

Instructions
1.   Take your dough and roll it out. Cut out circles from each large dough to make 4 personal pizzas (Dom uses a coffee can or a large soup container that you get in a Chinese restaurant).
2.   Add oil to a 12-inch frying pan, approximately 2 inches and begin to heat.
3.   Make sure oil is hot and then put the dough in. Cook on one side and flip it after it starts to puff up or brown.
4.   Flip it over and start adding the sauce and cheese and whatever other toppings you want on it.
5.   Let cheese start to melt.
6.   You'll know it's done when it starts puffing out. The dough becomes very airy and starts puffing out almost like a donut. It almost grows to the size of a piece of paper. It's really delicious!

Sonnie D's Asparagus Parmigiana

Serves 4-6

Prep Time: 10mins
Cook Time: 8mins OR until Golden Brown

2 bunches of asparagus
2 cloves of fresh garlic, pressed
Salt and pepper
Olive oil
1 ½ cups of parmigiana cheese

Instructions

1. Boil the asparagus for a few minutes until they are a little soft, but not too soft. Then plunge them into a pot of cold water to stop the cooking. This is called blanching.
2. Drain.
3. On a cookie sheet, line the asparagus up.
4. Drizzle olive oil over the asparagus. Sprinkle salt and pepper over it.
5. Spread the pressed garlic evenly over the asparagus.
6. Pour a cup and half of cheese over the asparagus.
7. Place under broiler but keep a close watch. This should be done in under 8 minutes or so.
8. When the cheese is golden brown, take it out and serve.

I learned this recipe from an old restaurant called Grotto D'oro in Sheepshead Bay, Brooklyn... sadly, it's no longer there. It was Dominick and mine's weekly date spot. When I tasted it, I had to make it at home. Classic dish at my table.

Savannah's Pernil & Potatoes

Serves 10-14

Prep Time: 15mins
Cook Time: 5-6hrs

10-12 lbs. of pork shoulder with at least half skin on

1 lb. of red potatoes

Approximately 12 cloves of fresh garlic

7 pouches of Sazon

2 tbsp of pepper

2 tbsp of salt

2 tbsp of oregano

2 tbsp of garlic Powder

2 tbsp of adobo spice

2 tbsp of paprika

Instructions

1. Cut up potatoes. No need to peel them, just wash.
2. Wash the roast and poke holes all over it.
3. Stuff garlic cloves in all the holes.
4. In a separate bowl, do equal parts of Adobe, paprika, garlic powder and pepper.
5. Add about 7 pouches of Sazon.
6. Add oregano.
7. Add water to make a paste.
8. Rub mixture all over the roast.
9. Put in roasting pan skin side down and seal VERY TIGHTLY with foil so no steam gets out.
10. Put it oven overnight like from 11pm to 7am at 200 degrees.
11. When you wake up, flip the roast. Should be skin side up now. If you are adding potatoes, cut them up into medium-sized chunks and add them into the pan.
12. Reseal tightly again, so no steam gets out.
13. Cook for about another 5 to 6 hours (check it at 5 hours).
14. The roast should be done, but turn oven up to 400 degrees and cook a little while longer until the skin is crunchy.

The potatoes are to die for! Enjoy!

Savannah loves this recipe! My cousin Fat Ang taught me this recipe. She used to have a deli in Staten Island and made it for her customers. They would come from all over for her pernil.

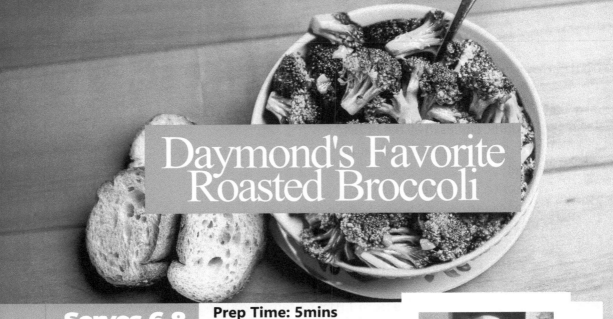

Daymond's Favorite Roasted Broccoli

Serves 6-8

Prep Time: 5mins
Cook Time: 10-15mins

2 heads of broccoli
6 cloves of garlic
Olive oil
Sea salt
Pepper

Instructions

1. Preheat oven to 400 degrees.
2. If you have a Wolf oven, like me, you can use the roast feature at 400 also.
3. Cut up the broccoli and only use the tree part, not the stems.
4. Put olive oil and garlic in a bowl (enough to coat but not soak broccoli).
5. Cover with the olive oil and add the whole cloves of garlic.
6. Add sea salt and pepper and toss to coat.
7. Put broccoli on cookie sheet flat and roast until tips start to turn dark brown.

This actually came to me on a whim. I made it for Daymond John. It was on a fourteen foot Christmas table when he came over for a party but he made a beeline for it. Daymond took a liking to my roasted broccoli. He loved it more than my lobster... and my lobster is FANTASTIC! He said it should be on a menu in a restaurant.

Baby Dom's Loaded Roasted Potatoes

Serves 6-8　　**Prep Time: 30mins**
Cook Time: 40mins

1 5-lb. bag of baby potatoes
2 sticks of butter
1 onion, cubed
1 16-oz bag of shredded Mexican cheese
1 cup of scallions, cut
1 cup of bacon, chopped
Olive oil
Salt and pepper to taste
Sour cream optional

Instructions

1. Preheat oven to 400 degrees. If you have a roast feature, use that.
2. Wash and slice each potato in half.
3. Cube your onion and add to potatoes.
4. Coat with olive oil, salt, and pepper.
5. Bake in oven until golden brown and slightly soft, or until you like the texture.
6. Put 2 sticks of butter in a bowl, sliced up.
7. Mix bacon and cheese together in a small bowl.
8. Take the hot potatoes out and throw them in the bowl with the butter until it's all absorbed.
9. Put the bacon cheese mix on top of potatoes.
10. Put bowl back in the oven for another 7 to 10 minutes until cheese is melted.

BE CAREFUL TAKING THE BOWL OUT OF THE OVEN. IT WILL BE VERY HOT.
Before Staten Island Hustle, I made Ronnie this when he was younger. He was growing at a crazy rate and I wanted to keep him full... especially when I was working at the school. He still eats it. My son, Baby Dom, always calls me the "Potato Whisperer" LOL!

Big Dom's Fish Salad

Something else I can't have due to my allergy to shellfish! I still love it, just can't have it... unless I want to go to the hospital. But like I said before, cook for your family, not for yourself.

Prep Time: 1.5-2hrs
Cook Time: This depends on your choice of seafood. see instructions for more details

3- 12 oz lobster tails
2 lbs. of extra-large shrimp
1 can of scungilli
1 can of real crabmeat
3 small octopus
2 lbs. of calamari cut and cleaned
5 stalks of celery into slices
3 fresh lemons
1 cup of fresh chopped garlic
1 bunch of parsley, finely chopped
Olive oil
Salt
Pepper
Red pepper flakes

Instructions

1.   In a large pot, boil some water with salt.
2.   For this recipe, I cook everything separately because the other items cook differently.
3.   First...take the shrimp, boil until pink. Take out.
4.   Put crabmeat and scungilli aside in another bowl. These don't need to be cooked.
5.   Cook lobster tails until white. Cool then cut the tail up and put in a bowl with shrimp, crabmeat and scungilli.
6.   Then, cook the calamari in the same water. Keep checking for softness. Cool the fish and add to bowl with the rest of the fish.
7.   Then add octopus in same boiling water and cook for four more minutes. Slice it up and add to bowl with rest of fish.
8.   Add olive oil, salt, pepper, red pepper flakes, and parsley. Mix well.
9.   Do not add lemon yet (the lemon can cook the fish more).
10.   Put mixed fish mixture in refrigerator until cold.
11.   When you take out to serve, then add lemon.

Enjoy!

Grandpa Albie's Stuffed Mushrooms

Serves 8-10

Prep Time: 25mins
Cook Time: 15-20mins OR until Golden Brown

18 large mushrooms
3-4 cups of Panko breadcrumbs
Parmigiana cheese
1 cup of grated parmesan cheese... you can use Perino or Romano,
just to give you a few ideas.
5 tbsp of olive oil
1 bottle of cooking marsala wine
10 links of sausage... take them out of the casing

6 scallions. I use white & green parts minced
4 cloves of garlic, minced
1 cup of Panko
1 large mascarpone cheese
1/3 cup of freshly chopped parsley
Salt and pepper to taste

Instructions

1.   Preheat oven to 350 degrees.
2.   Start by taking the stems out of the mushrooms. Chop them and set them aside.
3.   Peel your mushrooms.
4.   Put mushroom caps in a shallow bowl, add marsala wine & olive oil. Toss and set aside.
5.   In a skillet, coat the bottom of the pan, add sausage meat & crumble it with the back of a wooden spoon or use a meat masher (you can buy them on Amazon for cheap).
6.   Add the chopped mushroom stems and cook them for 3 minutes.
7.   Stir in scallions & garlic and cook them for 3 minutes, stirring occasionally.
8.   Add the Panko breadcrumbs, then stir them in, combining them with the other ingredients.
9.   Swirl in the mascarpone until it melts into a creamy mixture.
10. Turn off the heat, add your grated cheese, parsley, and all your seasonings to taste.
11. Cool slightly.
12. Fill each mushroom cap with the sausage mixture.
13. On a cookie sheet, line up your stuffed mushrooms in a single layer.
14. Pour the extra marsala wine over the mushrooms and bake till the mushrooms are brown and crusty.
13. Put them on a beautiful platter, serve, and enjoy! Delish!

Side Note: I've made this recipe and put the stuffing over macroni. OMG... it was a hit! TRY IT!

Queen Jeannie's Stuffed Artichokes

This was taught to me by my mother when I was 13. My mother was the "Queen of Stuffed Artichokes", so that makes me and Cheffy the Princesses, I guess. I added the caper juice to my recipe though (that's the big difference). OMG Jeannie, Cheffy, and I absolutely love it!

Serves 6

Prep Time: 30mins
Cook Time: 1hr

6 large artichokes
4 cups of breadcrumbs
Use a variety of grated cheeses. I use many different ones like Grand Padano, Parmagiano Reggiano and Cavicallo
Provolone cheese
6 cloves of chopped garlic
Olive oil
Salt and pepper
Fresh, chopped parsley

Caper Juice:
1 stick of butter
10 cloves of garlic, chopped
1 cup of capers
1 can of chicken broth
½ cup of white wine
Salt and pepper to taste
Red pepper to taste

Side Note: Know that capers will make the juice salty as it is, so be lenient on the salt until it's how you like it. Taste it and if you like it saltier, add salt.
If you like it spicier, add more red pepper flakes.

Instructions
1. In saucepan, add a stick of butter, and about 10 cloves of chopped garlic.
2. Cook on low until golden brown.
3. Be very careful not to burn. Burned garlic is just nasty!
4. Add a can of chicken broth.
5. Add 1/2 cup of white wine.
6. Add salt, pepper and red pepper.
7. Add cup of capers.
8. Keep cooking and stirring.

For the artichokes:
1. Cut the stems off the artichokes.
2. Cut the tops off too and trim the leaves so you have a square shape.
3. Put in a large pot of boiling water.
4. Add salt and boil until the leaves are soft. Sometimes this can take a while, but keep checking the leaves.
5. Meanwhile, in a large bowl, add 4 cups of breadcrumbs and lots of grated cheese.
6. Add salt and pepper and coat in olive oil.
7. When the artichokes are done, take them out of the water and drain.
8. Pull apart at the center of the artichoke and start to stuff them with the breadcrumb/cheese mixture.
9. For more cheesy goodness, I add a small piece of provolone cheese and sprinkle a little of the crumb mixture onto the leaves.
10. Put them in a roasting pan and pour the caper juice over the artichokes.
11. Cover the pan and put it in the oven, and cook for 30 minutes or so.
12. In the last 5 to 10 minutes, uncover and check to see if the crumbs are golden brown and baste one more time with the juice.

Audrianna's "Cheffy" Beef Goulash

Serves 6-8

Prep Time: 20-30mins
Cook Time: 3.5hrs

3 lbs. of cubed stew meat
10 beef bouillon cubes
2 large onions, sliced and cubed
10 carrots, peeled and cut into fourths
1/3 cup of olive oil
3 of the 12 oz. bags of broad noodles
3 sticks of butter
Salt and pepper to taste
Wondra Flour

Instructions

1. In a large sauce pot, add oil and heat until hot.
2. Add in onions and meat and stir until meat is brown and the onions are transparent.
3. Add carrots and toss carrots for about 3 minutes.
4. Add salt and pepper to taste.
5. Add the bouillon cubes and start adding water until meat is covered, approximately, 3/4 of the pot should be full.
6. Heat until a full boil, then set to simmer.
7. Simmer for about 3 hours, but stir every 30 minutes so it doesn't burn.

Cook the 3 packages of broad noodles and drain, then add all the butter if using all three packs.

Check meat, and when it's shredding, turn it off. To thicken the sauce in the pot, get a large glass of water and add Wondra flour (or regular) and stir until you see no lumps. Add to the boiling brown juice to thicken it.

I serve this with buttered noodles.

This dinner really comes in handy when you're a working mom. This can be put in a crockpot. Set it and forget it!

Cheffy absolutely loves this dish. And I'm teaching her early on how to cook it. And when it's time, she will carry the Detore torch in the kitchen!

Angel((a)
My Sister, My Friend:
Our Big Journey

JANINE DETORE

AFTERWORD

P.S. The (secret) meatball recipe is in our memoir. This was a promise I made to my sister not to give it up unless it was worth it! And our story is worth it.

Janine

CPSIA information can be obtained
at www.ICGtesting.com
Printed in the USA
BVHW011748061221
623349BV00009B/328